BAD JOBU – GOOD DAD

How Getting a Bad Dog Can Make You Better Dad

Manny Bartolini

COPYRIGHT

TABLE OF CONTENTS

INTRODUCTION

Congratulations! By opening this book you have demonstrated a willingness to become the best father you can be. I don't claim to have all the answers. I don't have a degree in child psychology, and no one has invited me onto a television talk show to discuss modern parenting.

That being said, I am the father of four children—three boys and one girl—and most of my education as a parent came from real life.

Oddly enough, some of the most important lessons came from a very small and very difficult chihuahua named Jobu.

When my wife and I first brought Jobu home, I thought we had made a terrible mistake. She was the size of a rat, barked constantly, and seemed incapable of learning even the simplest commands. I expected her to live for maybe a year or two before we quietly found her a 'better home.'

Thirteen years later, Jobu was still with us. Her behavior never improved. She never stopped barking. But, somewhere along the way, she taught me nearly everything I needed to know about being a good father.

This book is about fatherhood, responsibility, patience, and the strange ways life prepares us for the roles we are meant to play. Each chapter explores a lesson Jobu inadvertently taught me—lessons that made me a better father to my children.

If you're reading this, you're probably about to become

a father, or perhaps you already are one and searching for perspective. Either way, welcome. The journey ahead will test you, humble you, and transform you in ways you cannot yet imagine.

And, if you happen to have difficult dogs, pay attention. They might be teaching you more than you realize.

PROLOGUE

I'd like to explain a little about me, some background so you understand how ill-prepared I was to be a father. I am the youngest of five. I was a latchkey kid, who had little structure and few rules in my youth. Other than a few trips to visit family in Mexico and a school trip to Washington D.C., I had never been many places or experienced much. And though I was a good kid, I never really had any responsibilities. That all changed when I joined the U.S. Army.

At that point, my life took a massive turn, and I've often joked that I felt a bit like Forest Gump. I was blessed to do some very cool stuff. I attended the best leadership institution in the world. I rappelled down sheer cliffs. I jumped from perfectly good planes. I boxed and got hit in the face and gut. I gave shots and got stuck by needles. I learned to fly helicopters, fire weapons and blow stuff up. I completed sprint marathons. Interestingly, not once in all those awesome experiences did I feel like I lost control.

One day, I found myself at the veterinary clinic with a small puppy who had been with us one week. Jobu was her name. We were there to have the vet embed a tracking device under her skin. If ever she got lost, anyone who found her would be able to identify her owners and where she lived so we could get her back.

I was holding Jobu as the vet approached with the syringe. The needle was massive. The vet grabbed a fold of her skin and placed the tip against her. As she pushed the needle forward, she pushed too hard, and the needle exited on the other side of the skin fold. When she engaged the depressor, the chip—twice the size of a tic-tac,--landed on her coat.

Man, that was too much. I immediately got woozy. I was faint, my face and ears got hot. The room started to close in around me. I felt like I needed to take a seat. I felt like I was about to pass out for the first and only time in my life.

For the first time in my life I felt vulnerable, weak.

At that point in my life, if you had asked me to rank my priorities, I would have answered honestly: career first, family second, faith third. The Army had given me purpose and identity. Everything else fit around the mission.

Then we lost Lincoln.

***

Our first child, Lincoln, was stillborn at twenty-six weeks.

Nothing in my training—nothing in my life—had prepared me for that. I had jumped from aircraft, led men under pressure, and stayed calm through situations most people never face. But standing in that hospital room, holding a son I would never get to raise, I felt utterly lost. Weak. Incapable.

And the hardest part wasn't my own grief. It was watching Wendy suffer.

My wife was devastated in ways I could not fathom. She was hurting, raw, and easily wounded by comments people meant as comfort but landed like punches. "You'll have another baby," they would say, as if one child could replace another. She was sensitive in ways I had never seen—not because she was fragile, but because something sacred had been taken from her, and the world kept moving as if it hadn't happened.

I felt as though I had lost my connection with her. She was in a place I could not understand, and I did not know how to help. I could not fix this. I could not lead us through it the way I had led soldiers through a mission. This was not a problem with a solution. It was a wound that only time and God's grace could heal.

In that darkness, I turned to my faith. Not out of habit —out of desperation. And I found what I needed. I found comfort in knowing that God would hold me even when I could not hold myself together. That He was present in the silence and the grief. That even when I felt like I had lost everything, I had not been abandoned.

That experience rearranged my life. I rebuilt my priorities from scratch: faith first, family second, career third. It was not a small adjustment. It was a complete reordering—and it has made all the difference.

With faith as my foundation, I became a better husband. And becoming a better husband made me a better father.

***

I need to tell you about Wendy, because no honest book about fatherhood can ignore the woman who makes it possible.

Wendy has become the foundation of our family. While I travel for work and keep the bills paid, she manages everything that actually keeps a household running: the meals, the schedules, the doctor appointments, the school forms, the clothes, the holidays, the birthday parties, the family celebrations. She does it all—not because I asked her to, but because she chose this role and she excels at it.

As we said in our vows: she is our family planner and the one who nurtures our home. I keep the checkbook balanced, carve the Thanksgiving turkey and protect the family. We are a team. A good one.

I tell you this because fatherhood does not happen in isolation. The man you become as a father depends heavily on the partnership you build with your wife. Get that right, and everything else gets easier. Neglect it, and nothing else will compensate.

But before I understood any of that—before Lincoln, before the grief, before I learned to lean on faith and partner with Wendy—there was a three-pound chihuahua who started the whole education.

Her name was Jobu. And she had a lot to teach me.

GOT PATIENCE? — GET SOME!

Everything slows down when you become a father. Simple tasks suddenly become complex operations involving planning, supplies, and timing. Getting ready to leave the house transforms from a five-minute process into a thirty-minute ordeal involving diapers, bottles, backup outfits, and negotiations about which toys can come along.

Babies demand patience because their needs always come first. They don't care if you're running late for work or if you just sat down to eat. When they need something, they need it now, and they will make that need abundantly clear.

Before children arrive, you may think you are a patient person. I certainly did. I had served in the Army, completed multiple deployments, and considered myself calm under pressure. Then Jobu arrived.

My wife and I brought her home on a Tuesday afternoon, after our honeymoon cruise. Jobu was 1.6 pounds of pure chaos wrapped in tan fur. She barked at shadows, refused to be potty-trained, and had an uncanny ability to find the one spot on the carpet you had just cleaned.

"She's just a baby," my wife promised. "She'll calm down."

Months later, nothing had changed. Jobu still barked at

everything. She still refused to go outside when it rained. She still treated our home like her personal bathroom.

She was tiny, far too small to get up and down off the furniture by herself. She would bark to let you know she wanted you to lift her on the couch. You would pick her up with one hand and gently place her on the couch. Moments later, she would bark to inform you she wanted down. Again, you would pick her up with one hand and gently place her on the floor. She would repeat this cycle, much more frequently than I would like to admit.

To be honest, I was not a patient man. I yelled at the dog, as if that would change anything. I tried every training technique I could find online. I considered whether our local shelter had a "no questions asked" return policy.

Then our first son was born.

Suddenly, Jobu's constant needs seemed manageable. The dog, who had days before driven me to frustration, now seemed almost easy compared to a colicky infant who refused to sleep. When my son screamed for three hours straight at 2 AM, I remembered all those times I had lost my temper over Jobu's barking.

The difference was simple: I couldn't yell at my son. I couldn't lose my patience with a baby who was simply trying to communicate the only way he knew how. I had to breathe, stay calm, and figure out what he needed.

Jobu had given me practice. Every frustrating moment with that dog had been preparation for the patience fatherhood would demand. I just hadn't realized I was training.

Patience isn't about suppressing frustration. It's about understanding that some things cannot be rushed. Babies develop on their own timeline. They learn to sleep through the night when they're ready, not when it's convenient for you. They master skills at their own pace, regardless of what the parenting books promise.

The same was true for Jobu. She never became the obedient dog I wanted. But she did eventually settle into a routine we could both live with. It took years, not weeks. And it required me to adjust my expectations.

That's the real lesson of patience: accepting that the timeline isn't always yours to control. Your job is to show up consistently, provide what's needed, and trust the process—even when progress seems impossibly slow.

BABIES HAVE A LANGUAGE – LEARN IT

Babies cry. A lot. At first, it feels overwhelming. But, eventually, you realize that crying is simply communication. Hungry, tired, uncomfortable, bored: crying is the universal language of infants.

In those first weeks of fatherhood, the crying seemed endless and indecipherable. Every cry sounded the same to me! Each sound felt like an emergency. Was he hungry? In pain? Dying? My wife seemed to understand immediately, but I stood there feeling helpless and confused.

Then I remembered Jobu.

That dog barked at everything. The mailman. Squirrels. Leaves blowing across the yard. Her own reflection in the sliding glass door. At first, every bark sent me running to see what catastrophe was unfolding. I quickly learned that 95% of Jobu's alerts were false alarms.

Over time, I learned to distinguish between her different barks. The "someone's at the door" bark was sharp and insistent. The "I see a squirrel" bark was high-pitched and repetitive. The "I need to go outside" bark came in short, urgent bursts.

Learning Jobu's communication system prepared me for

decoding my son's cries. The hungry cry was rhythmic and demanding. The tired cry built slowly from fussy to frantic. The uncomfortable cry was sharp and immediate.

More importantly, I learned that not every cry required panic. Sometimes, babies cry because they're processing their day or learning to self-soothe. Sometimes dogs bark because they're seeking attention, or they hear something you don't. The key is learning to read the signals and respond appropriately.

My wife noticed the difference. "You're getting really good at calming him down," she said one evening after I had successfully settled our son after a difficult day. "How did you figure that out?"

"Jobu," I said.

She laughed, but it was true. That neurotic little dog taught me to listen beyond the noise. She taught me to stay calm when the alerts started. She taught me that communication doesn't always come in words, and that patience plus attention eventually reveals the pattern.

This lesson extended beyond infancy. As my children grew, they developed new ways of communicating distress. Toddlers have tantrums. School-age children get quiet and withdrawn. Teenagers get frustrated and retreat to their rooms.

Each stage requires learning a new language. But the fundamental skill remains the same: pay attention, stay calm, and learn to decode what they're really trying to tell you.

The ability to decipher their language is a gift, even when it doesn't feel like one. It's your child's way of saying, "I need you." Your job is to learn their language and respond.

YOUR HANDS WILL GET DIRTY

I did some cool stuff while I was in the U.S. Army. A lot of it involved getting dirty. It never bothered me when it was part of my job. Mud, sweat, spider webs, gun powder and bloody cuts were common. I remember when I was getting combat lifesaver qualified, my friend Michael Hunt (don't call him Mike!) and I gave each other saline IV's. I watched as the needle entered my arm and it was no big deal.

However, once I was off the clock, I think I may have been clinically OCD. I washed my hands all the time. I never touched my face. I was obsessive about my foot care regimen. I probably drove my wife crazy with how over the top I was with concerns about biology and germs.

Which brings us back to the importance of accepting biology when raising children.

Parenthood introduces you to the realities of biology in ways no biology class ever could. Diapers, spit-up, and unexpected messes become normal parts of life. Things that would have made you gag before children now barely register.

I learned this lesson from Jobu, though I fought it every step of the way.

Jobu was never successfully house-trained. We tried everything—crate training, puppy pads, taking her outside every hour, reward systems, training classes. Nothing worked. That dog had a bladder the size of a thimble and the stubbornness of a mule.

For the first year, I was disgusted. Every accident sent me into a cleaning frenzy, scrubbing carpets and spraying odor eliminators. I wore gloves. I held my breath. I complained constantly to my wife about the injustice of it all.

“It's not that big a deal,” she would say, calmly cleaning up another mess. “She's not doing it to frustrate you."

I didn't believe her. How could a creature that small produce so much chaos? It was as though she was doing it on purpose.

Then our first son arrived, and I discovered that babies are biological chaos machines that make dogs look pristine by comparison.

The first diaper blowout happened at 3 AM on our third day home from the hospital. Our son had managed to completely cover himself, his clothes, his blanket, and somehow his hair with what seemed like an impossible amount of biological material.

I stood there in shock, holding this screaming, filthy baby, and thought: “This is way worse than Jobu.”

But something surprising happened. Instead of being disgusted, I just... dealt with it. I cleaned him up, changed his clothes, washed the blanket, and got him settled. No hesitation. No gagging. No gloves.

My wife watched from the bed, too exhausted to help. “Good job, daddy,” she said.

I realized then that Jobu had prepared me. All those months of cleaning up after a three-pound dog had built up my tolerance for the biological realities of caring for another living creature. By the time my son needed me to handle truly messy situations, I was a seasoned veteran.

Responsibility replaced squeamishness. When you love someone—whether it's a difficult dog or a helpless baby—their needs matter more than your comfort. You don't think about whether something is gross. You just handle it and move on.

This lesson extended beyond diapers. Sick children vomit. Teething babies drool. Toddlers explore the world by putting everything in their mouths and occasionally sharing those discoveries with you. I went to work on more than one occasion with clothes that bore the signs of parenthood.

Fatherhood requires getting your hands dirty—literally and figuratively. It means dealing with situations that aren't pleasant or pretty. It means doing what needs to be done, even when it's uncomfortable.

Jobu taught me that biology doesn't care about your preferences. Life is messy. Love means showing up for the messy parts without complaint.

SACRIFICE DOESN'T MEAN YOU LOSE

Before children, weekends and evenings often belong to you. You make plans based on your schedule, your interests, your energy level. Time is a resource you control.

After children, those hours belong to someone else.

I learned this gradually, starting with Jobu.

Before the dog, I spent my weekends how I wanted. Morning runs. Afternoon projects in the music room. Evening games with friends. My time was mine to allocate.

Jobu changed that. She needed to be fed on a schedule. She needed to be let out multiple times per day. She needed attention and exercise and supervision because she couldn't be trusted alone for more than an hour without destroying something (like a bathroom wall!!).

My basketball nights became shorter. My Saturday mornings now included a dog walk before I could do anything else. Weekend trips required finding someone to watch her, which was unsurprisingly difficult given her difficult personality.

I resented it at first. "This is supposed to be my time," I would think while walking Jobu in the rain instead of watching the game I had been looking forward to all week.

But gradually, something shifted. Taking care of Jobu became part of my routine rather than an interruption of it.

I stopped thinking about what I was giving up and started accepting this new reality.

When our first child arrived, the sacrifices multiplied exponentially. Sleep became a luxury. Hobbies became memories. Social life contracted to a small circle of other exhausted parents. The things I used to guard jealously—my time, my sleep, my freedom—now belonged entirely to a tiny human who demanded everything.

Yet the sacrifices rarely felt like losses. Watching my son learn to smile, laugh, and eventually walk became more rewarding than any hobby I had abandoned. Reading bedtime stories replaced watching sports highlights. Teaching him to ride a bike mattered more than maintaining my own cycling routine.

The practice I got with Jobu made the transition easier. I had already learned that caring for another creature meant putting their needs first. I had already discovered that sacrifice becomes easier when you love someone.

Here's what no one tells you about sacrifice: it stops feeling like sacrifice when you see the results. Every late night you spend comforting a sick child, every weekend soccer game you attend instead of sleeping in, every vacation you plan around their interests instead of yours—these become investments rather than losses.

Jobu never knew she was teaching me. But every time I gave up something I wanted to take care of her, I was training for fatherhood. I was learning that love means choosing someone else's needs over your own convenience.

The sacrifices are real. The time, the sleep, the freedom—you will give these up. But what you receive in return makes the trade worthwhile.

Fatherhood is a long series of small sacrifices that add up to something profound. Jobu taught me to make those sacrifices without resentment.

DISCIPLINE IS NOT A BAD WORD

At the midpoint of this book, you would probably assume that I never enjoyed Jobu's shenanigans. On the contrary, I often found her very entertaining. She is, without question, the smartest dog I have ever known. Though she never took to any formal training, she had extraordinary street smarts.

Jobu had a stepsister named Tamale, a sweet dachshund who loved every person she ever met. Though Tamale was more than double Jobu's size, she had roughly one-tenth of Jobu's mental capacity. Despite their many differences, they shared a common love for rawhide sticks.

With a small mouth and tiny teeth, Jobu often struggled to chew the rawhide well enough to bite off a chunk. Tamale, however, had no such difficulties. She would quickly gnaw them into soft, easy-to-tear strips.

When the girls got their snacks, they would each run to separate corners of the living room—which is when Jobu would hatch her devious plan. She would wait until Tamale had softened the rawhide to the perfect, bite-sized consistency she craved.

Then, without warning, Jobu would sprint to the window and start barking furiously at nothing. Tamale, simple as she was, would drop her rawhide and charge toward the window, barking at the same imaginary threat that Jobu had just invented. The moment Tamale arrived at the window, Jobu would wheel around, sprint back, and steal the perfectly chewed rawhide Tamale had worked so hard to prepare.

It worked every single time.

And every single time, I took the stolen rawhide from Jobu and returned it to Tamale.

I admired the hustle. Honestly, part of me was impressed—the scheme was borderline genius. But I wanted to establish a principle, even with two dogs who would never fully understand it: hard work is a prerequisite to ownership, and eventually, to enjoyment. You don't get to take what someone else earned just because you're clever enough to figure out how.

That same drama repeated itself, almost scene for scene, when my boys came along.

Swap Tamale's trusting nature for a younger brother who hadn't yet learned to guard his work. The older one would build an elaborate distraction—"Hey, come look at this!"—and the moment his brother's back was turned, he'd swipe the piece he wanted. Stuffed animals were another battlefield. One brother would spend twenty minutes arranging his guys in a specific formation, and another would casually walk by and grab the best one as if it had always been his.

Every time, I intervened the same way I had with Jobu and Tamale. The stolen piece went back. The explanation was simple and consistent: "Your brother built that. If you want one like it, build your own."

They didn't always like it. Jobu never liked it either. But that is the nature of discipline—it is not designed to be popular. It is designed to teach.

Many new fathers struggle with discipline. We want to be the fun parent, the one our children run to rather than away from. The idea of setting firm boundaries feels harsh, especially with young children who don't yet understand why the rules exist.

Many new fathers struggle with discipline. We want to be the fun parent, the one our children run to rather than away from. The idea of setting firm boundaries feels harsh, especially with young children who don't yet understand why the rules exist.

But discipline is not punishment. It is communication. It is structure. It teaches children how to navigate the world safely and respectfully. Without it, they struggle to understand boundaries, consequences, and the connection between their choices and their outcomes.

The training classes we attended with Jobu emphasized consistency above all else. The same command had to mean the same thing every time. The same behavior had to receive the same response every time. Jobu needed to know what to expect.

It didn't work perfectly—Jobu never became a model of obedience—but it worked enough. She learned that certain behaviors were not acceptable. She learned that some boundaries were non-negotiable. And most importantly, she learned that the rules were consistent, not arbitrary.

When my first son reached toddlerhood, the same principles applied. He needed to know what was expected. He needed consistent responses to his behavior. He needed boundaries that kept him safe and helped him understand how to function in the world.

I watched other parents struggle with discipline, alternating between permissiveness and anger. One day they would let a behavior slide; the next day they would explode over the same action. Their children seemed confused and anxious, never sure what to expect.

Jobu had taught me that consistency was the key. If hitting was not allowed, it was never allowed—not even when it seemed playful, not even when I was tired, not even when it appeared harmless. The rule had to be the same every time.

This didn't mean being harsh. It meant being clear. When my son broke a rule, the consequence was immediate but calm. No yelling, no shaming, no anger—just a consistent response that reinforced the boundary.

"How do you stay so patient?" another father asked me at the playground one afternoon, after watching me calmly redirect my son several times.

"Practice," I said. "Lots of practice with a very difficult dog."

Discipline is not about control. It is about teaching your children to regulate themselves, make good choices, and understand that actions have consequences. The boundaries you set when they are young become the internal compass they use when they are older. The consistency you provide becomes the stability they can count on. The discipline you maintain becomes the self-discipline they develop.

Jobu needed discipline to feel secure. Children need it for the same reason. It is not about being strict or authoritarian—it is about providing structure in a chaotic world.

The firmness you show today becomes the foundation they build on tomorrow.

PROVIDING COSTS MORE THAN YOU EXPECT

Before Jobu arrived, I thought having a dog would be inexpensive. A bag of food every month, maybe some toys, an occasional vet visit. Simple.

I was spectacularly wrong.

Jobu had expensive taste in dog food—the cheap stuff made her sick. As a puppy, she needed regular vet visits because she was prone to infections. Vaccinations were annual, and more expensive than I imagined. She destroyed toys faster than we could replace them. She required special grooming products despite her short hair. And dental cleanings cost more than the rent at our first apartment.

The financial costs added up, but they were manageable. The real expense was everything else.

Time. Energy. Attention. Mental bandwidth. These were the currencies Jobu demanded most, and they were far more valuable than money.

She needed to be walked twice a day, rain or shine. She needed supervision when guests visited because she was not trustworthy around strangers. She was too small to get on the couch, and too small to get down when she was on the couch. She needed someone home every few hours because she couldn't hold her bladder longer than that.

These requirements shaped my schedule, my choices, my entire lifestyle. We couldn't stay late at work without arranging care for her. We couldn't take spontaneous weekend trips. We couldn't do anything without first considering: What about Jobu?

When children arrived, the investment multiplied by a factor of ten.

The financial costs were real—diapers, pumps, cribs, car seats, childcare, medical expenses, clothes they outgrew every three months. But again, money was not the most expensive part.

Children require everything you have. Every ounce of energy, every minute of free time, every bit of creative problem-solving ability. They need you at 2 AM and 6 AM and throughout the day. They need your patience when you're exhausted, your attention when it's depleted, your love when you feel empty.

The practice I got with Jobu made this slightly less shocking. I had already learned that providing for another creature means organizing your entire life around their needs. I had already discovered that the real cost isn't measured in dollars—it's measured in everything else you have to offer.

But here's what surprised me: the investment pays returns you never expected.

Every hour you spend reading bedtime stories becomes a foundation for their love of learning. Every dollar you spend on experiences with them becomes a memory they'll carry forever. Every moment of attention you give becomes security they can draw on for the rest of their lives.

The investment is enormous. You will give more than you thought you had to give. You will sacrifice things you once thought were essential. You will reorganize your entire existence around these small people who need you.

And somehow, it will be worth it.

Jobu taught me that providing isn't just about money. It's about showing up consistently, even when it's inconvenient. It's about putting someone else's needs on equal footing with your own. It's about investing everything you have into someone who can never fully repay you.

That's fatherhood: an investment so large you can't calculate the return, but one you make willingly anyway.

PRIDE IN YOUR CHILD > PRIDE IN SELF

I never expected to feel proud of a dog.

Jobu was not an accomplished animal. She never learned impressive tricks. She would not sit. She was horrible on the leash. She was never well-behaved enough to take to public places. She failed basic obedience training multiple times.

But one afternoon, something shifted.

A friend came to visit with her young daughter. The child was about two years old and immediately wanted to pet Jobu. They always did!! I hesitated—Jobu was not good with strangers, and children made her especially nervous.

But before I could intervene, Jobu walked calmly over to the little girl and sat down. The child petted her gently, and Jobu stayed completely still, patient and calm in a way I had never seen.

"Wow," my friend said. "She's so good with kids."

I felt an unexpected surge of pride. This difficult, neurotic, badly-behaved dog had shown a moment of grace. She had been gentle when it mattered. And I was proud of her.

That feeling was nothing compared to what fatherhood would bring.

The first time my son recognized me and smiled, I felt pride. When he took his first steps toward me, I felt pride. When he shared his toy with another child at the playground, I felt pride.

Every small accomplishment—learning to tie his shoes, reading his first book alone, standing up to a bully—filled me with a fierce joy I had never experienced before.

But the deeper pride came from unexpected moments. Not the big achievements, but the small choices that revealed character.

When my second son was born with jaundice, my oldest —then only 3 years old—brought his favorite stuffed animal to the hospital. "For baby," he said solemnly, placing it on the incubator. "So he won't be scared."

That moment of compassion from such a young child brought tears to my eyes. I was proud not because he had accomplished something impressive, but because he had shown kindness when someone needed it.

Jobu had given me a preview of this feeling. She had shown me that pride isn't always about grand achievements. Sometimes it's about witnessing a moment of unexpected grace from someone you care about.

As a father, you will feel pride in a thousand small moments. The first time your child says "please" without prompting. The time they apologize to a friend they've wronged. The afternoon they choose to help you instead of playing with their toys. When a teacher or an elderly couple that dined at the restaurant table next to yours compliments you on how well-behaved your child is, you will swell with pride.

These moments accumulate into something larger—the recognition that you are raising a person of character. Someone who makes good choices not because they have to, but because they want to.

Few feelings compare to watching your child succeed, whether that success is mastering a difficult skill or simply choosing kindness over convenience. Pride in their accomplishments becomes one of the most rewarding parts of fatherhood.

Jobu taught me to notice these moments. She taught me that pride doesn't require perfection. It just requires presence—being there to witness the small triumphs and the unexpected grace.

Your children will make you proud in ways you cannot yet imagine. Pay attention. Those moments are the rewards for everything you've invested.

PROTECTION IS HARDWIRED

Fatherhood awakens an ancient instinct—the desire to protect your children from harm. It becomes automatic and powerful, often surprising in its intensity.

I first felt this with Jobu, though I didn't recognize it at the time.

Despite all her flaws, Jobu was mine to protect. She was tiny—never more than six pounds. When a neighbor's much larger dog got loose and came charging toward us during a walk, I didn't think. I scooped Jobu up with one hand and put myself between her and the threat. The other dog was probably friendly, but it didn't matter. Something primal kicked in. I had to protect her.

When my first son was born, that protective instinct multiplied a thousandfold.

The first few nights home from the hospital, I barely slept. Every sound startled me awake. Was he breathing? Was he too hot? Too cold? I found myself checking on him constantly, driven by an anxiety I had never experienced before.

My wife noticed. "He's fine," she would say gently. "You need to sleep."

But I couldn't. The need to protect him was overwhelming. This tiny, helpless person depended entirely on me to keep him safe. The weight of that responsibility felt immense—especially after losing Lincoln. I had already learned, in the worst possible way, that you cannot protect your children from everything. That knowledge did not reduce the instinct. It amplified it.

I remember purchasing two gallon-size hand sanitizer dispensers. If anyone wanted to hold our son, I made them sanitize their hands first. When he was born, whooping cough infections were on the rise in California, where our extended family lived. I told every family member who wanted to meet our firstborn that they needed to be vaccinated. No exceptions. Some thought I was overreacting. I didn't care.

As he grew, the threats changed but the instinct remained. Toddler-proofing the house became an obsession. I saw danger everywhere—sharp corners, electrical outlets, stairs, windows, doors. Every object became a potential hazard that needed to be secured.

My friends found it amusing. "You've got the whole house wrapped in bubble wrap," one joked during a visit.

But I couldn't help it. Protection wasn't just about physical safety—it extended to everything. I worried about his emotional well-being, his social development, whether other children were kind to him at daycare.

One afternoon at the playground, an older child shoved my son off a swing. He fell and scraped his knee. Before I knew what I was doing, I had crossed the playground in about three strides and was standing over my son, every muscle tensed, glaring at the other kid.

The other child's father appeared immediately. "Hey," he said, hands up, voice calm. "Let's be cool. They're just kids."

He was right. And in the two seconds it took him to say it, I recognized what had happened. Rational thought had left the building and pure protective instinct had taken the wheel. My son wasn't in danger. He had a scraped knee. But every fiber of my body had reacted as though someone had threatened his life.

I took a breath. I unclenched my jaw. I knelt down, checked my son's knee, and told him he was fine. Then I looked at the other father and nodded. "You're right. We're good."

That moment taught me something Jobu alone could not: the instinct to protect is real and it is powerful, but it needs a governor. An uncontrolled protective impulse doesn't make you a strong father. It makes you unpredictable. And your children are always watching.

My son didn't need me to intimidate another kid on the playground. He needed me to show him how a man handles a situation—with composure, not rage. He needed to see that strength includes the ability to stand down.

That's when I understood the fuller lesson Jobu had been teaching me. The practice runs with her—the protective impulse that kicked in when she was threatened—had been preparation for the overwhelming drive to protect my children. But protection alone is not enough. You have to control it.

Children need to experience age-appropriate risks. When they learn to walk, sometimes they fall. The truth is, they need to fall sometimes, to build resilience. They need to navigate social conflicts and develop problem-solving skills. They need to develop their own instincts for self-protection.

The challenge of fatherhood is balancing protection with independence. You must keep them safe while also allowing them to grow. You must guard them from genuine dangers while letting them face the small risks that build competence and confidence.

While they are young, you will choose the people with whom they interact. You may find that the parents you meet at swim lessons, or on the soccer team, or at preschool are people with whom you genuinely enjoy spending time. But if the children of those parents are undisciplined or cruel, you may have to end a friendship you valued in order to protect your child. That is a sacrifice. Make it without hesitation.

With four children now, I have learned to moderate that fierce protective instinct. I still feel it—every time one of them is hurt or threatened, the same automatic response kicks in. But I have learned to pause, assess the situation, and respond rather than react.

Jobu taught me that protection is hardwired. It is not a choice. When you love someone, you will defend them without thinking. But she also taught me—through her own neurotic fears of shadows and strangers—that overprotection can be its own kind of harm.

Your job is to keep them safe while teaching them to protect themselves. The instinct to shield them will be powerful. Learning when to let them face challenges on their own will be one of your hardest lessons.

UNCONDITIONAL LOVE

The final lesson Jobu taught me was about love. True love isn't conditional. It doesn't depend on good behavior, accomplishments, or meeting expectations. It shows up on good days and bad days alike.

Jobu never became the dog I thought I wanted. Thirteen years later, she still barked too much, still had accidents in the house, and still ignored basic commands. By any objective measure, she was a badly-behaved pet.

But somewhere along the way, I stopped caring about her flaws. She was an extension of me, family. Her quirks became endearing rather than infuriating. The things that once drove me to frustration now just make me smile.

This shift happened so gradually I almost didn't notice it. One day I realized I loved that difficult little dog, not despite her problems but including them. She was who she was, and that was enough.

That realization prepared me for the most important aspect of fatherhood.

Your children may disappoint you. They will make mistakes, poor choices, and decisions with which you disagree. They will not always meet your expectations. They will sometimes frustrate, confuse, and worry you.

But your love cannot be conditioned on their perfection.

My second son struggled at bedtime. Despite every intervention and strategy we tried, separation and nighttime came hard to him. Watching him struggle was painful. I wanted to fix it, to make it easier, to see him succeed in the ways I wanted.

But one evening, after another difficult bedtime session, he looked up at me with tears in his eyes and asked, "Daddy, are you mad at me?"

The question broke my heart. In that moment, I thought of Jobu—of how I had learned to love her exactly as she was, not as I wanted her to be.

"Never," I told him. "I love you. I am proud of you. I just want you to go to sleep because I am tired too."

And I meant it. He was my son. His struggles didn't diminish my love—if anything, they deepened it. Watching him persevere despite difficulty made me respect him more, not less.

Unconditional love means showing up consistently, regardless of circumstances. It means your children know they can count on you even when they fail. It means your affection doesn't depend on their achievements.

This doesn't mean accepting poor behavior without consequence. It doesn't mean abandoning expectations or standards. But it means your love remains constant even when you're disappointed, frustrated, or worried.

Jobu taught me this lesson through sheer persistence. Year after year of difficult behavior should have eroded my patience. Instead, it deepened my affection. I learned to love her for who she actually was, not who I wished she would become.

Jobu taught me this lesson through sheer persistence. Year after year of difficult behavior should have eroded my patience. Instead, it deepened my affection. I learned to love her for who she actually was, not who I wished she would become.

That's the essence of fatherhood: loving your children for exactly who they are while helping them become the best version of themselves. Accepting them completely while still guiding them forward.

Your children will test this love. Teenagers especially seem designed to push every boundary and question every certainty. They will make choices you don't understand. They will temporarily become people you don't recognize.

But your love must remain steady. It must be the one thing they can count on, even when everything else feels uncertain.

***

Jobu got older. She slept most of the day and moved slowly when she did get up. She still barked, though not as loudly. She still had frequent accidents. She was still, fundamentally, the same difficult dog she had always been.

The last day I saw her, she was frail. She was unable to stand comfortably on her own. She had lost control of her bladder, and had not eaten in days. The veterinarian told me she had lived a good life, and she thought it might be the right time to say goodbye.

As she lay on the stainless steel table, wrapped in one of her favorite blankets, I was reminded of all the wonderful memories that included her. I held her in my hands as her body relaxed. Her eyes closed as I gently stroked her wonderfully large ears. As she took her last breath, my throat tightened. Tears ran down my cheeks as I wept uncontrollably. I held her still, little body for 20 minutes, unable to talk, and unwilling to leave.

I loved her.

That love—deep, steady, patient, unconditional—is

what she taught me to give my children. It's the most important lesson of all.

Your children need to know that your love isn't earned or conditional. It simply is. That certainty becomes the strong foundation upon which they will build their lives.

CONCLUSION

Jobu never knew she was my teacher. She was just being herself—difficult, demanding, and stubbornly resistant to change. Yet in being exactly who she was, she prepared me for fatherhood in ways I could not have anticipated.

Every lesson she taught me—patience, communication, accepting biological realities, sacrifice, discipline, provision, pride, protection, and unconditional love—became essential to raising my four children.

The irony is not lost on me. I never wanted a dog. At times, I wished we had never brought Jobu home.

Now I recognize Jobu as one of the best things that ever happened to me and to our family.

If you're reading this as a new father or father-to-be, you're probably feeling a mix of excitement and terror. That's ok. Fatherhood will test you in ways you cannot yet comprehend. It will exhaust you, humble you, and sometimes make you question whether you're capable of the job.

You are capable. Not because you're perfect, but because love makes you capable. The same way my love for a difficult dog taught me patience and sacrifice, your love for your children will teach you everything you need to know.

The lessons will come from unexpected places. Pay attention and stay engaged. Life has a way of preparing us for what comes next, often through circumstances we wouldn't have chosen.

Maybe for you it won't be a dog. Maybe it will be a different challenge—a demanding job, a difficult living situation, a relationship that tests your patience. Whatever form the preparation takes, recognize it for what it is: training for the most important role you'll ever play.

Thirteen years after Jobu came into my life, I'm grateful for every frustrating moment. Every mess cleaned up, every sleepless night spent listening to her whine and bark, every sacrifice made—they were all investments in becoming the father my children deserved.

Your journey will be different from mine, but the fundamentals remain the same. Show up consistently. Love unconditionally. Be patient with the process. Accept that perfection is impossible, but growth is guaranteed.

And if you happen to have a difficult dog, thank her. She might be teaching you more than you realize.

Welcome to fatherhood. It's the hardest job you'll ever love.

ABOUT THE AUTHOR

Manny Bartolini is the father of four children—three boys and one girl—and a former Army officer. He studied economics at the United States Military Academy and served multiple deployments before transitioning to civilian life.

He learned most of his parenting lessons the same way many fathers do: through trial, error, and a surprising amount of help from a very small, very difficult dog named Jobu.

He lives with his wife, children, three dogs, three tortoises and a leopard gecko in their home, where he continues learning that fatherhood is less about having all the answers and more about showing up consistently with love.

This is his first book.

"But as for me and my household, we will serve the Lord."

Joshua 24:15, NIV

www.ingramcontent.com/pod-product-compliance
Lightning Source LLC
LaVergne TN
LVHW011053110826
845149LV00015B/3485

9798995866619